SEXY LAUNDRY

by

MARIOS ELLINAS

For worldwide distribution. Printed in the U.S.A.

ISBN: 978-0-692-97152-9

Sexy Laundry

By Marios Ellinas

Printed by Createspace

Copyright © 2017 by Marios A. Ellinas

www.mariosellinas.com

maellinas@hotmail.com

Cover photo (front) and cover design by **Sergio Barrera**

Cover photo (back) by **Caitlin Reynolds**

To Danielle Marie

ACKNOWLEDGMENTS

Heartfelt thanks to:

JM Olejarz for editing the manuscript

Sergio Barrera for the cover design and front cover photography

Mark DeJesus for formatting

Caitlin Reynolds for back cover photography

Ashley Wu for transcription of talks

Son of Thunder Publications for transcription and distribution

Danielle, Christos, Caleb, and Chloe — the best family I could have hoped for

The leaders and congregation of Valley Shore for their constant support

My parents for their unconditional love and for always having my back

Contents

INTRODUCTION

The human race has produced many remarkable accomplishments. Cities, medicine, technology, diplomacy, wonders of architecture and engineering, the arts — truly an innumerable array of achievement; a most astonishing display of greatness. Though our progress as a species has been astounding, it has also been limited. We have come far, but not far enough. We are operating nowhere near full capacity.

For as long as we claim to have resided here, we have sustained a handicap. Our growth and development have always been stunted. We have not collectively maximized our potential, because we have never properly recognized and valued half of the human race: women.

Historically, voices have risen from many corners of the world to address gender inequality and women's rights. Some were tempered, others extreme; some were heeded, others stifled. Much positive change has taken place, and today women are generally treated better than ever before. But not as equal partners to men, not as invaluable assets to humanity.

This purpose of this book is neither to catalog areas of inequality nor to point the finger at *man*kind for misperceiving and sidelining women. Rather, it is to present a picture of what is available for everyone if we adjust our mindset to recognize that women's authority and contributions are equivalent to men's.

For decades, I have drawn much inspiration from the women of the Bible: Deborah's prophetic insight, Jael's decisiveness, Ruth's loyalty, Rahab's faith, Esther's courage, and the outstanding character of several Marys (including the mother of Jesus) mentioned in the four Gospels and the book of Acts. But there is one individual who embodies most of the virtues exemplified by these and many other women from the biblical narrative. She is not a specific individual with a name and story, but a type of Woman: the virtuous woman of Proverbs 31.

Proverbs 31:10-31. Twenty-two verses that feature Woman—the ideal counterpart to Man, operating in the fullness of our Creator's original design for her and demonstrating what's possible for men, families, cultures, nations, and civilizations when she is honored, empowered, heeded, and celebrated. In these verses we find Woman as she was always destined to be — powerful. In God's heart there was neither desire nor intent for Woman to be dominated by Man. The plan was that she would exercise dominion *with* him. Her nature and faculties, though in many ways different from Man's, complement his. And when Woman and Man work together harmoniously, there is no limit to their potential.

I wrote this book because I heard the Proverbs 31 Woman (whom I will refer to as 31W) calling out to us. She is issuing a summons to every one of us. It is an invitation to consider the unattained heights of achievement and fulfillment that are available to humanity through her example and the impartation from her life. A call to embrace Woman for who she is and everything she is capable of. Woman is not to be perceived and treated merely as a doting wife, a nurturing mother, or even a career professional — though such endeavors are honorable and noteworthy. And she most certainly is not to be observed as a sex symbol and exploited as an object of lust. Woman, fearfully and wonderfully made, is Man's equal partner in humanity's God-given assignment to rule over everything He created.

CHAPTER 1:

MARKED

She made a right turn into the driveway, the tires of her SUV crunching against the gravel. The household's dogs started barking, because everyone, even one of their masters, would be treated as a potential intruder until their canine olfactory systems said otherwise. Putting the car in park, she gathered a few belongings from the passenger seat. She was still on a business call, which she transferred from the vehicle's speakers to her mobile before opening the door. She stepped out of the car, one hand pressing the phone to her ear, the other carrying her purse and a few small bags. A familiar fragrance greeted her. The unmistakable smell of drying laundry, emanating from a vent near the front door. While uttering instructions and final greetings to her caller, she stopped and looked in the direction of the vent. Another whiff of the atmosphere that Bounce dryer sheets had helped create. She smiled to herself and entered the house from a side door by the kitchen. "Hey, babe, I'm home!"

* * *

I was born with a birth defect on my face, a prominent birthmark. My loving parents continually affirmed me, saying the birthmark made me very special, but other people had a different perspective. A deep red-and-purple mark beneath my eye generated curiosity at best, with frequent questions asked, such as "What did the other guy look like?"

Growing up on the small island of Cyprus did not help. Not only were people generally awkward toward individuals with visible blemishes, they were also superstitious. If not openly, then certainly in the back of their minds, they were asking questions similar to the one Jesus' disciples asked him when they encountered a man blind from birth: *"Who sinned, this man or his parents, that he was born blind?"* (John 9:2)

My birthmark made things especially difficult when it came to girls and dating. Throughout adolescence, when many young men become interested in members of the opposite sex, and explore the possibilities of relationships, I seemed doomed to the status of "strictly friend." Girls frequently told me that although they enjoyed my company and respected me immensely, they could see me only as a buddy—maybe even as a brother—but not as a boyfriend. As my children say, I was perpetually "friend-zoned."

Through my leadership gift, my participation in sports, and my outgoing personality I was able to build many friendships with girls, but none progressed to romance. And as it was clear to everyone—including Cypriot girls' highly protective parents—that things would never go beyond friendship, my female classmates felt safe to open their hearts to me. Dreams, aspirations, fears, problems—I heard it all. Ironically, some of them even asked me how they could date my handsome teammates. Once, when an eager young woman was turned down by one of the guys (in spite of my excellent advice), I found the courage to suggest a consolation prize—me. Not only was my offer met with an emphatic *no*, but the girl refused to talk to me for months, simply because I dared to conceive of the notion of us dating.

In spite of all the pain my birthmark caused, it proved to be a blessing in disguise. A combination of girls' confidence in me as a safe friend, and my acceptance of the impossibility of ever going out with them led me to appreciate girls for more than their physical appearance. In a way, I was lucky to see the young women for who they really were, and I began to develop a mindset that would serve me well in the years to come.

I remember quite a few locker-room conversations with the guys when, at the mention of various "hot chicks" and their astonishing features, I would contribute my own unique perspective — things such as, "You know, she has some great ideas about the ever-shifting central European geopolitical environment" or "Her poetry reveals amazing depths of soul." Needless to say, I was not celebrated among the guys as a locker-room sage.

Due to my birthmark, by default, I learned to value and respect women at a young age, and by the time I graduated college I had enjoyed many wholesome and genuine relationships with classmates and peers, many of which have lasted through the years.

As a student of history, I cannot find a time period or culture in which women have *not* been represented as being inferior to and weaker than men. I attribute much of the gender inequality, and especially the oppression of women worldwide, to this misperception. My rather unique and painful upbringing, as it pertained to my female peers, enabled me to circumvent the erroneous mindsets that have always tainted men's view of women. Had women deemed me attractive, or "boyfriend material," I am fairly certain I would have entertained similar notions. I would not have appreciated women's inner qualities, nor would I have recognized their true place among us. Instead of seeing women as different but equal counterparts to men, I, like most of the guys, would have relegated women to the task of holding support roles; worse yet, to the emotional and sexual gratification of men.

In 1991, while in my dorm room at a college campus in New Jersey, I had a significant encounter with Yahweh, the God of the Bible. He appeared to me in a dream and lovingly called me into relationship with Him and to His service. Everything changed after that, and continued to, through a number of similar mystical encounters with invisible heavenly realms and beings. I have endured much scrutiny and criticism for that part of my spiritual walk, and to this day many question the validity of my claims. I choose not to defend myself, but trust that the fruit from my life will reflect heaven's input, especially the ceaseless transformational work of the Holy Spirit. I state this here because you, the reader, will have to choose whether you accept this next part.

I have had numerous spiritual experiences in which I felt closeness and connection to female biblical figures. During times of prayer and meditation in the Word, I have had several encounters with Esther, Deborah, Mary the mother of Jesus, and others. I have also had several powerful interactions with someone I believe to be Wisdom, as Solomon knew her and wrote of her in Proverbs: a female angelic entity whom I perceive to be the Spirit of Wisdom mentioned in Isaiah 11. Yet none of these female beings have affected me as much as the woman of Proverbs 31.

When I first read about 31W, my heart started beating faster. It felt as though I was reading about someone real—someone with whom I was already acquainted. Though it was clear from the text that 31W is not a specific person, I felt that she was, and that somehow, during the course of my life, she and I had already built a measure of relationship. She had qualities I had already seen in some of my female classmates from high school. She carried herself similarly to my female study partners from college. Most of all, she was in most ways everything I adore and admire about my wife, Danielle. I believe that I felt this way because 31W was Woman—the female counterpart to Man—the way I had grown to perceive her through my spiritual encounters.

In short, I recognized 31W, but I also felt she recognized me. I bowed my head toward her with respect; she nodded in my direction with approval. Many spiritual encounters later, I felt it was time to share some of my views about Woman. Not through the clichéd and, as we will see later in this book, misguided sermons about her on Mother's Day. 31W was too important for me to incorporate into a sermon. But our relationship was too precious to keep to myself.

In His infinite goodness, God masterfully utilizes the shards of our broken lives to fashion some of His most beautiful handiwork. As the Savior, Jesus Christ redeems all of us, every part of us—our past, present, and future. Through much prayer and reflection I came to the realization that the Holy Spirit had been using the stirrings that surrounded my encounters with 31W to redeem my birthmark experience. God was pointing out that the respect and honor I had cultivated toward women during those painful years had given me the insight to speak authoritatively about 31W, to present Woman to the world for who she really is. I'm very thankful for the opportunity to introduce her to you, and I trust she will inspire you as well.

CHAPTER 2:

HOUSEWIFE?!

"Settle down, boys," he commanded the dogs from the upper level of the house. She couldn't see him but knew he was in their bedroom. "Hey, babe," he said, stepping out of the room. He walked down the stairs with a plastic bag in his hand and kissed her on the cheek. "Be right back. Throwing out some garbage." She placed her things on an empty chair in the living room and took a quick inventory of the surroundings. The table had been set and red wine had been poured into two glasses. He reappeared in the kitchen and started washing his hands. "Steaks are almost ready," he said, raising his voice over the noise of the faucet. Then he dashed toward the sunroom with an empty platter in hand. "I think you'll love these cuts I got from Walt's." She smiled and shook her head playfully. Picking up one of the wine glasses, she swirled the deep red liquid around for a few moments and took a sip. "Mmmm!"

* * *

One of the greatest mistakes of Scriptural exegesis and biblical interpretation has been the presentation of the Proverbs 31 Woman as a good housewife. For me, describing her as such is tantamount to saying that tennis legend Serena

Williams is athletically inclined. As we will see below, there is a degree of truth in 31W being a housewife — but keeping house is only one star in her constellation.

Of course, there's nothing wrong with being a housewife. I honor every woman who chooses to raise a family and who focuses her efforts on building her home. What I do not agree with is presenting such a calling as being the most viable option available to women, as though that is the pinnacle of what Woman can achieve. I disagree with labels that limit women, and I particularly dislike for preachers to interpret the exceptional feats of someone like 31W as good housekeeping.

Labels can be misleading. They foster misperceptions. We humans are complex by nature and manifold in function, and we live and work in ever-changing, fast-paced environments. No title, prefix, or suffix by our names can adequately describe us; yet, we tend to gravitate toward labels. Within a few minutes of making a new acquaintance, we ask, "What do you do?" And as the person describes their work, we begin to print the seemingly appropriate label in our minds.

"Who was that man you were talking to, honey?" a woman inquires of her husband during the ride home from a dinner party.

"He's a chef. Works at a New York bistro."

"I wonder what he thought of the truffle risotto," she said. "Seemed a bit overcooked to me."

The moment we place a label on someone, we begin to perceive that person according to our (often limited) understanding of their field of endeavor. The chef may also have been a widower, the sole parent of four children since his wife's untimely passing shortly after the birth of their youngest daughter. He may have started a humanitarian organization with classmates at the age of 16. He may have logged enough hours to be a pilot of commercial aircraft, though choosing to fly only recreationally. But to the couple driving home from the party, he was nothing more than "the chef."

Year after year, when Mother's Day sermons and keynote speakers at women's conferences highlight 31W's homemaking abilities, we do not receive an accurate picture of who Woman is and the value she adds to those around her. Nor do we properly assess her potential. 31W supersedes the label of wife, mother, and most certainly of housewife — though I reiterate respect for such callings. As the rest of this book points out, 31W is an outstanding individual of competence and character, a woman whose lifestyle and values continually make a way for her to exercise her divinely granted authority.

Let us begin to look into 31W's life.

"Who can find a virtuous wife? For her worth is far above rubies. The heart of her husband safely trusts her." (Proverbs 31:10-11)

The portion of this chapter of Proverbs that deals with 31W opens with a general statement about her worth, and then a brief reference to her husband — one of three in this segment. I call him the Proverbs 31 Man, or 31M. A later chapter deals with him in more detail.

Before 31W's stated greatness is elaborated on, we are told "her husband safely trusts her." In other words, the man closest to the woman worth more than rubies has full confidence in her integrity. To me it reads like this:

You are now approaching the realm of 31W. She is astonishing. Don't be afraid or insecure around her – even when it becomes apparent she outdoes you. Her very husband is quite comfortable with it all.

If men would understand and heed this verse. First and foremost, this is not the biographical summary of a specific person, but the description of Woman the way God fashioned her in the beginning. The Bible indicates that God made Adam out of the dust of the earth and Eve out of Adam's rib (Genesis 2:21–23). Before Adam and Eve fell, they were assigned the task of ruling the earth as equals. They differed in physical stature and physiology, but their assignment was one and the same: to "have dominion over the fish of the sea, over the birds of the air, and over the cattle, over all the earth and over every creeping thing that creeps on the earth" (Genesis 2:26). God created them, and he equipped each of them with qualities that would complement each other in their world-keeping responsibility. In the spiritual realm, Man and Woman are equals and co-laborers in the exercise of dominion. The mistake that humanity, and especially the Church, has made repeatedly is to let the differences between men and women in the flesh obscure their equality in the spirit. In other words, the inequalities we have fostered between sexes in the natural realm reflect our ignorance of their joint status in the spiritual realm.

Most preachers interpret "safely trusts her" as an affirmation of 31W's marital fidelity. One minister said, "That means she's faithful; she doesn't cat around on him." These are superficial and expedient remarks, stemming from a place of bigotry and insecurity, not discernment.

The Christian Church has all too often addressed the need for sexual purity from a place of fear. Early on in my ministerial journey, during many ecclesiastical meetings, my peers and I were exhorted to operate with utmost integrity as it pertained to women. No problem with that—I agree. Sooner or later in the seminar or teaching, the speaker would quote 1 Thessalonians 5:22 and emphasize that we must do everything possible to "avoid the appearance of evil." That included adopting practices such as having our wives or a female staff member present when counseling a woman, or at least keeping the door cracked open throughout the meeting — I guess so everyone else in the office could be assured their leader wasn't having an affair in his study during office hours.

Throughout most of my years as a follower of Christ, I have found that admonitions and warnings regarding men's lustfulness are overemphasized, while other important truths are neglected — for instance, the powerful statement that "to the pure all things are pure" (Titus 1:15). In fact, in the context of ecclesiastical leaders' constant harping on the purity issue, the rest of the verse is intriguing: "...but to those who are defiled and unbelieving nothing is pure; but even their mind and conscience are defiled." Could it be that my peers and I, who were forced to endure session after session on the subject, weren't the ones with the issue, but rather that the incessant cautions originated in the speakers' own challenges with the matter? It has often proved to be the case that some of the fieriest morality preachers suffer moral failures — sometimes during the very same seasons in which the sexual purity messages are being proclaimed.

Hypocrisy is not the most reprehensible variable in the "avoid-the-appearance-of-evil" pulpit. A greater issue lies in the fact that platforms are established out of the fear of failure instead of the exaltation of our God-given capacity for holiness and wholesome living. For far too long, avoiding the appearance of evil has been pursued at the expense of demonstrating and exemplifying the appearance of good. In other words, we have always played defense in this area, and in doing so have limited men and women in their interactions. Instead of encouraging generations of young men to cultivate lasting Kingdom relationships with their sisters in God, we have sown tares of fear and mistrust — of themselves and each another — in their lives. Moreover, Christian men and women have often missed the opportunity to relate to each other in a way that would provoke and inspire the world at large to pursue godly standards.

For many years now, Danielle and I have enjoyed relationships with friends and colleagues of the opposite sex. These relationships have played a large role in our personal development; moreover, they have been strategically significant in our work. We can both say we would not be where we are today without them. Danielle and I don't listen in on each other's calls, don't check each other's emails, and don't "leave the door cracked." God trusts us, and we trust each other—we are empowered by that trust, and we are stewards of it. Walking in trust is much better than fear; growing in wholesome Kingdom relationships is preferable to avoiding people because we don't trust ourselves or them.

A few years ago our family lived for two years in the mountains of Cyprus. We lived in a mission community with friends of ours from Gateways Beyond International. The organization's leaders and some of the staff families lived on the island year-round. There were many occasions, in the course of our life in the mountains, when one of us would need a ride to the nearest town, 30 minutes away, and the only person available to drive was someone of the opposite sex. The teachings about guarding against appearances of evil would most likely have condemned our collaboration and support of each other as brothers and sisters through our sharing of rides; however, it was never an issue for us. We operated out of covenant relationships and the highest standards of integrity. We strongly believed that our associations and friendships glorified God and enhanced our Kingdom bonds as families. In more than 25 years of Gateways mission communities around the world sharing life together, never once has there been an incident of impropriety of any kind. To the pure, all things are pure, and we do well to focus on living out that truth.

The reference to 31W being "safely trusted" has little or nothing to do with marital fidelity; rather, it sets the stage for what is coming next — the featuring of 31W's attributes of greatness. 31W's husband has full confidence that his wife, who is in every way Woman according to God's original blueprint, is capable of ruling alongside him. As the next verse states, *"She does him good and not evil all the days of her life"* (Prov. 31:12). As we are about to see, Woman leverages all the freedom and support from her union with a secure husband to be outstanding, not only by way of morality, but also in everything she becomes and accomplishes.

CHAPTER 3:

WOMAN!

She found the steaks delicious and perfectly cooked, and the 2009 Bordeaux he had selected was an ideal pairing. It had been a lovely, quiet meal. The kids were out with friends; the dogs were lying down near the table, hoping for leftovers of grilled bovine. Between bites and drinks the couple traded stories about their workdays. For her it had been a nonstop ordeal, from the moment she arrived until quitting time. Phone calls, meetings, filings. She had even eaten lunch while tapping away at her laptop. "How about you?" she asked, raising her glass to her lips. "Oh, you know," he said, "the usual. Some writing in the morning and then a series of Skype calls. I came home in the afternoon to…" She reached over and placed her hand on his. "You've been a busy guy around here," she said, nodding at the platter on the table and then at a pile of folded laundry on the living room couch.

*   *   *

I recently watched the motion picture *Wonder Woman* with my wife. It was generally a good flick, but the first few minutes were awesome! Several scenes at an idyllic island depicted strong, honorable, and remarkably fit women who were engaged in intense training and education, all for the purpose of stewarding and governing their domain. As the music was building during a fight scene, and one warrior was releasing an arrow from her bow in midair, I thought of the Proverbs 31 Woman.

The Bible is replete with examples of outstanding womanhood, but there is only one description of a woman who has it all—31W. She is the personification of the invaluable asset God added to the universe when he created Woman. And though she may not have Wonder Woman's superpowers, 31W has all the necessary attributes to administer God's grace and power to her generation. Let us look at some of her areas of endeavor and the character qualities they demonstrate:

She seeks wool and flax, and willingly works with her hands. (Prov. 31:13)

31W is both industrious and creative; she manufactures items for home use and commerce. Her search for the proper raw materials for her craft is a good indicator of her high standard for excellence. Not just any wool and flax will do. It is also important to note that she does her handiwork willingly, not out of obligation or coercion.

She is like the merchant ships. She brings her food from afar. (Prov. 31:14)

There are undoubtedly food items nearby—a garden, a local market, perhaps, yet 31W partakes in national and probably international commerce for even the barest of necessities. Woman was designed, like Man, to see the big picture. To explore realms of possibility and availability within the vastness of God's wonderful creation. International commerce provides much more for humanity than the exchange of goods and services. It broadens our horizons and bolsters our identity as God's heirs—joint heirs with Jesus Christ. When we trade with other regions and nations, we exercise our privilege to cooperate with fellow heirs within God-given jurisdictional realms. For example, interacting with a Swiss watchmaking company during a search for a new watch is an acknowledgment of the preeminence of those heirs in fashioning excellent timepieces. Furthermore, we grow in respect and honor of other cultures when we acquire "food from afar." We learn to negotiate. We adapt. We adjust. We advance our skills in both diplomacy and communication, and at times even in resolving conflicts. In short, we expand and grow in key areas of life and godliness. Woman looks beyond her horizons for the basics of life, because she understands the growth component in such pursuits.

And she also rises while it is yet night, and provides food for her household and a portion for her maidservants. (Prov. 31:15)

Even though 31W is far more than a housewife, her dedication to that role is given validity in this verse. It is not the entire truth of her, but it is true that 31W diligently looks after her family. While continually spreading her wings in the marketplace and beyond, she also ensures the proper running of her household — family and servants alike.

One reflection about servants: I have been blessed with many relationships in nations where having servants is customary. Some members of my extended family employ servants as well. I am always touched when the heads of such homes treat their servants with respect, when they include and look after them as members of the larger household.

She considers a field and buys it; from her profits she plants a vineyard. (Prov. 31:16)

This verse has two fascinating implications: First, 31W has the business acumen to make a real estate purchase on her own. Second, she makes the real estate purchase on her *own!* The absence of Man from this picture is notable. In considering the field, 31W may have sought input or advice from her husband—we do not know her exact process—but one thing is certain: She does not need her husband's permission or presence to make the purchase. Imagine this interaction around the dinner table on the day she closed the deal:

"So how was your day, love?"

"Great—I bought us a field. How was yours?"

Men must give women the freedom to explore, discover, and conquer. Women must take the initiative that is granted and, for the benefit of the entire household and even society at large, take the lead.

From her profits she plants a vineyard. (Prov. 31:16)

Sometimes nuggets of revelation can be found in what is not stated in a passage. Verse 16 comprises two declarative sentences. Consider the first one, ending with "and buys it," then look at the start of the next line, "From her profits." The semicolon between the two statements holds valuable information for us regarding 31W. After all, "It is the glory of God to conceal a matter, but the glory of kings to search out a matter" (Proverbs 25:2).

Profit is generated when something is sold for more than the purchase price. It is evident here that 31W bought a field with the intent of turning a profit by selling it. Which means she had knowledge of both the buyer's and seller's real estate markets. Moreover, if the sale of the field, as implied in the verse, occurred shortly after her acquisition of it, 31W would have had to negotiate a low purchase price to begin with in order to maximize her profit through the turnaround sale. But that's not all; she leveraged her profit from the field transactions to plant a vineyard, a completely different type of business venture altogether — demanding expertise, not only in real estate, but also in agriculture. She had to close the real estate deals and then "plant a vineyard," thus embarking on a wine-producing venture from the ground up.

From my observation of Danielle while we were raising our three small children, I concluded that God created Woman with a remarkable capacity for multitasking — an ability that is important for a mother when her eight-year-old is building a fort with some of dad's tools outside; her six-year-old is "cooking like mom" in the kitchen; and the four-year-old is using the hair dryer and mom's makeup to dress the doll that has just received a bath in the sink. All while the mother is cooking (real) dinner on the stove, tidying up the house, and washing a load of laundry in the basement.

Obviously, a mother's multitasking ability is essential for the well-being of her household in the scenario above. As admirable a quality as this is, Woman—and everyone around her—may be limited if her multitasking remains confined to the home.

Again, many women find their calling in the home, and I honor that, but generally speaking Woman must be empowered by society—and especially by her husband—to act on other fronts as well. I remember when it became clear to me, as the leader of our church, that my greatest asset, in terms of leadership, was my wife. The congregation grew quickly, as did my international speaking platform. I knew I needed someone to oversee the various ministries and walk closely with those who led them. I looked to Danielle's capabilities for handling many things well at the same time. The kids were grown and attending school. She had the time, and she certainly had the skill. Through a process, many times not easy (see Chapter 5), I gradually released responsibility to Danielle. I attribute much of the success that followed to her.

She perceives that her merchandise is good. (Prov. 31:18)

This is such a key verse. 31W recognizes the value in what she contributes. The relationship she has with Yahweh, the support she receives at home, and the respect she has earned in the marketplace enables 31W to see herself for who she really is, and to operate optimally in her spheres of giftedness and desire.

A woman who is well supported and aligned emotionally will not be insecure or competitive. She will not second-guess herself. She will not compare her accomplishments or her children's to those of other moms and their kids at the bus stop. And she will not feel intimidated when a strikingly beautiful woman walks into the room. She knows she is remarkable. She is affirmed in being so. She perceives that her merchandise is good.

She extends her hand to the poor. Yes, she reaches out her hands to the needy. (Prov. 31:20)

In the final chapter I describe a season of our lives during which Danielle was radically transformed, through encounters with God, into the woman she was always meant to be. As in the case of 31W, when Danielle was awakened to her true identity, she looked beyond the needs of her household. She began to pursue benevolence.

Early in 2009 Danielle formed a humanitarian organization to help children. She began by serving needy children and families in our own town. Today, through Danielle's efforts and those of her dedicated leaders, the operations of Radiant Destiny International have expanded internationally. It should be noted here that I was not at all involved in the establishment and running of this organization. My participation was limited to periodic financial support from my spheres of influence.

She is not afraid of snow for her household, for all her household is clothed with scarlet. (Prov. 31:21)

Fine linen denotes excellence, especially in the color purple — which was a true luxury in Bible times. Being able to afford fine things is one aspect of excellence; having a spirit of abundance and generosity to buy it without guilt is equally important.

For many years I was told by trusted advisers and confidants that owning certain brands of cars, watches, pens, and clothes was too extravagant and could be deemed pretentious. I disagreed. For me, owning material possessions has always been a matter of the heart. I believe if we remain humble about owning fine things, and we can afford to do so, then we can be free to buy the very best.

It is a tribute to the goodness of God and his rich blessings that I own almost everything I was once told not to consider. I will never apologize for it. I have friends in Horsham, England, who brilliantly coined the phrase "It's our daily bread" in reference to even the most extravagant of luxuries. We eat well when we are together; we stay in nice places; we shop for quality products. It's our daily bread, and we give glory to our Father in the way we steward such things.

31W's household is clothed with scarlet because of her proper mindset about wealth and her excellent, industrious lifestyle.

She makes tapestry for herself. Her clothing is fine linen and purple.

She makes linen garments and sells them, and supplies sashes for the merchants. (Prov. 31:22, 24)

Not only does she buy nice things, but she also designs them. She would not just shop for brand names; she would establish her own. 31W is dressed well and clothes her family in quality; furthermore, she occupies a unique niche in the clothing market by selling linen garments and accessories even for her fellow merchants. As a Cypriot friend in the restaurant business once told me, "You know a good restaurant because other restaurant owners eat there." 31W is not only doing good business, she is also esteemed and influential among her peers in the marketplace.

Long before I began to serve God and engage with the principles that govern His Kingdom, I was intrigued by this portion of Scripture:

Through wisdom a house is built, and by understanding it is established; by knowledge the rooms are filled with all precious and pleasant riches. (Prov. 24:3-4)

Those three forces — wisdom, understanding, and knowledge — are catalysts for the acquisition of resources and the increase of a person's stature and influence in the world. So much so that this statement comes without any conditions of faith or obedience. God isn't even mentioned in this portion. Believers and unbelievers will thrive and prosper if they grow in these areas.

31W's dealings are diverse and multifaceted, and she thrives in all she does because her dealings reflect large measures of wisdom, understanding, and knowledge. And through her dedication to God and His ways, 31W receives inspiration and motivation from the greatest force in all of creation: love. Achievement for the sake of notoriety may not stand the test of time. There must be a higher calling than making a name for ourselves or providing for our families. I believe God brought us into this world for a higher purpose: to demonstrate all the multifaceted attributes of His heart. According to the Bible, three virtues transcend space and time: "And now abide faith, hope, and love, but the greatest of these is love" (1 Corinthians 13:13).

CHAPTER 4:

HONORING AND HONORABLE

She gently squeezed his hand, slightly tilting her head. "The dogs are fed, the floors are swept, the kitchen is clean, the dishwasher is empty. You made dinner for us, set the table, and this — so good," she exclaimed, raising her wine glass a few inches. "Most of the laundry is done, too — and folded. There's probably even more I don't know about, isn't there?" she said. He smirked and took a sip of his wine. She got up from the table, taking his hand and leading him to the two neat stacks of clothing on the couch. She placed her hand on one of the piles and said, "This is so sexy."

"Sexy? What's sexy?"

"The laundry...the clean house...the meal. All of it — it's sexy to me."

* * *

I have spent countless hours studying and meditating on the subject of honor. I have taught about it in small gatherings and huge events in many nations. Truly, honor is an inexhaustible theme, because it is an expression of love. The Bible says God is love — that He and love are one and the same. When we engage with honor, to carry it and live by its standard, we function within the very folds of God's heart.

Honor is a high level of respect that is bestowed on us for our accomplishments, our position or status, the value others ascribe to us, and the inheritance we leave behind. 31W is a woman who is honoring and honorable. She gives and receives honor. And she does it well. She honors her children and even her servants by "watch[ing] over the ways of her household" — basically, by caring and providing for them. She honors heaven by "open[ing] her mouth with wisdom" and speaking "the law of kindness" (verse 26). And she generates much honor for her husband, contributing significantly to his reputation. Because she is honoring, he is "known in the gates, when he sits among the elders in the land" (verse 23). In every facet of her life, 31W releases honor from her heart to add value to those around her.

Because honor is an expression of God's love, 31W's example reveals God's heart and nature to everyone who knows her. 31W is limitless in potential, because God is; she is wise, caring, compassionate, industrious, creative, outstanding in her character and dealings, because God is. In Him she lives and moves and has her being. In God. In love.

God's love is 31W's driving force, her chief motivator. She has encountered and received God's love; she thrives in His love; she releases love in her household and to the world around her. She is not engaging with projects and completing tasks merely out of obligation or with a performance mentality. A higher purpose is being served.

An entire life of notoriety and achievement can be unfulfilling. The apostle Paul wrote to the Corinthian church that without love, the understanding of mysteries, all knowledge, spiritual gifting, self-sacrifice, miracles, and even martyrdom would be as a "resounding gong or clanging cymbal" (1 Corinthians 13:1–4).

Woman has an extraordinary capacity for love and honor. She can nurture her children; she can stand beside her husband; she can care for her colleagues, friends, and everyone else who has a place in her heart. As we saw in the last chapter, she can even reach out beyond her household to help the poor and needy. But for Woman's love to flow effectively into all these areas, she must be properly honored. She will love best when she is most loved. I am not suggesting that her love goes forth on a conditional basis; rather, that everyone who benefits from Woman's love should honor and love her in return.

We cannot fully honor what we don't love, and we cannot fully love without being honored. At our church we have a policy regarding speakers. Whoever is talking to the congregation, whether it is one of the pastors or a first-time guest speaker, is introduced by a member of our leadership team before coming up to the podium. Something honorable is said, and everyone is encouraged to receive the speaker with applause or a standing ovation. The practice is not so much to introduce the speaker—that is unnecessary for house regulars like me—but to establish an honoring environment. We have learned that all speakers do better if they are honored before their delivery.

Woman has the qualities within her to be honoring toward everyone around her; in turn, it is our responsibility, as Woman's colleagues, to ensure she also feels honorable—that she is esteemed and valued for her character and contributions.

Again, 31W models the possibilities. She is honoring, but she is also honorable. She gives and receives honor. There is a cause-and-effect element involving 31W and honor. As a reward for pursuing a lifestyle of honoring others, she is held in high regard by those she honors.

The Proverbs 31 Woman is praised and honored by her children, her husband, and by the author of the Proverbs 31 chapter, King Lemuel. The king's writings have been preserved for posterity, for all to read, and through them 31W has a lasting legacy.

Legacy is the form of honor that most appeals to me. There is one prayer I have uttered more than any other. It stems from the first part of John 15 and goes like this: "God, let my life bear fruit, fruit that remains." I consider being honored generationally — long after we depart this earth — the greatest honor, because whoever honors us after we pass on no longer has anything to gain from it. People who honor our status or achievements during this life may do so to obtain something from us. Honoring our legacy is more impartial; thus, it carries more weight.

There is one place in the world where the concept of legacy is continually before me when I visit: Singapore. The nation's first prime minister, Mr. Lee Kuan Yew, left Singapore a most remarkable inheritance, one I find unrivaled by any other leader in modern history.

Through his charismatic leadership and exceptional character, Mr. Lee helped establish Singapore as an independent country in the early 1970s. Then for several decades he and a dedicated group of leaders worked ceaselessly to transform Singapore — a country without any notable natural resources — from fishing villages and mud huts to the thriving, internationally renowned metropolis it is today. The country went from third-world to global dominance in finance, architecture, housing development, and many other areas—and all accomplished in one generation.

Mr. Lee worked remarkably hard to build up Singapore, but he also focused much effort on personal development. For example, he took lessons to improve his Mandarin until his last days. While making great strides in government and international politics, Mr. Lee became known worldwide for his uncompromising values as a statesman, but also as an outstanding husband, father, brother, and friend. I have watched interviews with Mr. Lee's siblings and closest confidants, who affirmed that power and influence never corrupted Lee Kuan Yew. He remained committed and faithful to all his relationships at all times. One of my favorite stories is of Mr. Lee sitting by his wife's bedside every night until her passing in 2010, reading her favorite poems to her after she suffered a stroke.

It is my conviction that we would be hard-pressed to find another world leader in history who accomplished so much in such a short time, leaving a great legacy.

When Mr. Lee passed away in March 2015, the entire nation mourned. Condolences streamed in from every corner of the world. Many world leaders attended the funeral presided by Mr. Lee's son, Lee Hsien Loong, who succeeded his father as prime minister. The wait for Singaporeans paying their respects while Mr. Lee's body lay in state at Parliament House was more than three hours long for three days straight. I watched the funeral online and wept through most of it, not out of mourning so much as being overwhelmed with inspiration.

Are we inspired by 31W? Does Woman model attributes that all of humanity should aspire to emulate? I believe she does. The extent to which she can succeed hinges in large part on the measure of support she receives. The more honoring that people are toward Woman, the more honoring and honorable she becomes.

*   *   *

She was enjoying a glass of Perrier with a lime, and watching a Netflix show with her daughter, who had come home a few minutes earlier. Having completed the kitchen and dining room cleanup, her husband was sitting by the table tapping away on his phone. "Whatcha doing, babe?" she asked.

"It's morning in Asia. Touching base with some of our peeps over there," he responded.

She blew him a kiss and kept watching the show. His daughter turned and caught his eye, then nodded and winked. She knew when mom was happy with her man. Kids…they always know.

Chapter 5:

Proverbs 31 Man

He stretched, interlocking his fingers and raising his arms toward the ceiling. Then he yawned and rubbed his eyes. "I think I'll head to bed, ladies," he said on his way to the stairs.

She paused the show and turned to look at him. "You're going to bed already?" she said with a chuckle. "It's only 9:30!"

"I know. I'm beat. Long day, I guess. Plus I..."

"What?"

"Well, tomorrow, I have to get up at 4:30."

"For what?"

"To hit the gym by 5:00. To work on this," he said, running his hand over his torso. "So that maybe someday...I can become sexier than laundry!"

*　　*　　*

I like the Proverbs 31 Man. I truly want to be like him.

Most of Proverbs 31 is dedicated to a presentation of the virtuous wife—who as I have discussed also represents Woman. For the most part her husband is absent from the picture, and for good reason. This tribute to 31W by King Lemuel is not about him. Many men try to finagle praise for themselves from even the slightest recognition that is directed toward their wives. 31M is very secure when the spotlight isn't shining on him. He is comfortable with barely being mentioned; yet he has a huge part to play in the empowerment of his wife.

Let's take another look at verse 11: "The heart of her husband safely trusts her..." We have already addressed misconceptions about this verse, and we have seen that 31M's trust extends to a lot more than his wife's marital fidelity or general honesty in her dealings. The next word in the verse is evidence to that effect: "...so he will have no lack of gain." "So," meaning *in order to*, or *so that*. Cause and effect. One action procures a certain result. The result is that 31M will maximize his gain—not just profitability in business, but in every area of life. He will be successful. He will increase. He will be victorious, because by trusting his wife, 31M supports her in reaching her fullest potential for greatness.

I gave a talk once about the Proverbs 31 Woman. Most people enjoyed the presentation, and were even inspired by it, but one man was unhappy. He approached me while I was walking to my car, and in a highly confrontational tone he said, "Women are supposed to submit to us. Don't give them an easy out like that." He chuckled nervously at first and then straightened his face to indicate this was no joke. I was neither amused nor intimidated by this man and his remark; rather, I was saddened that my talk had not made the least difference in his life. More of the same — that is what he'd get, and what the rest of humanity would get, if we adopted his mindset.

Since that day, others have expressed similar concerns. I have even had the occasional call in which well-meaning friends begin with, "Hey, Marios, are you OK?" Within a few minutes I realize the purpose of the call is to "reach out" to me and save me from my heretical leanings. "Marios, the Bible is clear on this…it's the Word of God, man." Then they quote Bible verses like this one:

Wives, submit to your own husbands, as to the Lord. For the husband is head of the wife, as also

Christ is head of the church; and He is the Savior of the body. (Ephesians 5:22–23)

Women submitting to men. That one. Let's deal with it, shall we?

God created woman to co-labor with man in the administration of his creation — to govern, to have dominion over everything. As *equals.* As discussed earlier, Man and Woman in their first estate, before the fall, were in perfect harmony, both in relationship and in the delegation of responsibility. They honored each other and carried out their tasks from the same perch of authority before the Father.

Any consideration of women submitting to men has to be placed within the context of this very equality in the spirit that God originally intended — otherwise the premise is built on a faulty foundation.

> *Her husband also, and he praises her. "Many daughters have done well, But you excel them all." Charm is deceitful and beauty is passing. But a woman who fears the Lord, she shall be praised. (Prov. 31:28–30)*

What woman would have a hard time with Ephesians 5:22 — in the context of co-laboring and co-ruling as equals — if her husband honored and praised her; if he served her; if he acknowledged that his success and influence were derived from the excellence that marked her life?

Women submitting to men may be in the Bible, but it is also conditional; it hinges on attitudes of the heart and on mindsets. The man who stopped me outside the church undoubtedly wanted to be able to pull out the "I'm the boss around here" card. When he couldn't have his way in one area of marriage or another, he intended to "pull rank" and set the record straight. Bad attitude, wrong mindset. I promise you it doesn't work that way.

But let's move on for a moment. Might women object less strenuously to Ephesians 5:22-23 — the verses about wives submitting to husbands — if those of the "submission persuasion" also factored in Paul's exhortation for husbands?

Husbands, love your wives, just as Christ also loved the church and gave Himself for her..." (Ephesians 5:25)

I've heard it more times than I care to remember: "Brother, I'd die for my wife—she knows I would. I do love her as Christ loved the Church. If anyone ever tried to harm her, I'd give my life for her." Some guys then get into specifics, which quickly start to resemble something from the Rambo, Rocky, and Bourne movies. And all I want to say to them is, "Spare us, man. Please spare us the macho talk, and while you're at it, spare us the false interpretation of Scripture."

Here's the problem: We often focus so much on the sacrificial aspect of Christ's love for the Church that we miss an equally important result from His death and resurrection. Jesus didn't die for us *only* to make a way for us to be saved. He sacrificed his life for our empowerment as well. Because Christ loved the Church, He sent her the Holy Spirit, who would give believers power and authority. Consider these statements Jesus made to His disciples before he left them in charge of the work He had begun in this world: "If I depart, I will send Him [the Holy Spirit] to you" (John 16:7); "But you shall receive power when the Holy Spirit has come upon you; and you shall be witnesses to Me in Jerusalem, and in all Judea and Samaria, and to the end of the earth" (Acts 1:8).

One more thought about submission. At the church I am honored to lead, I work alongside a number of great leaders. Each of us has a unique personality and set of skills. We also have unique areas of responsibility in the organization. On Tuesdays we come together for a staff meeting. A long time ago we established that the church's senior leader would rarely if ever lead the meeting, so every week the head of a different department leads it. This model affords everyone the opportunity to grow in leadership. Moreover, it is an exercise in submission and honor. Regardless of the position each of us holds in the church, we all learn to humble ourselves and honor the leader of each meeting. Our submission is never out of fear or subjection to a pecking order. We submit to one another in order to properly govern the church and advance God's Kingdom values through our proceedings.

I have never once had to assert myself as the leader of the church in any meeting, be it in a small group setting or the wider body. If I ever did have to do so, that would be the moment my influence would weaken in this particular body.

It is the same with marriage. If a husband feels he can tell his wife to submit to him, it is not because he has authority in the marriage, but because he has lost some of it.

A husband who loves his wife as Christ loved the Church is not merely the protector of and provider for his wife. He is the facilitator of the very environment in which she can thrive. He lays down his life for her to fulfill her destiny, and he celebrates her every step of the way, especially when she outdoes him.

I have a wonderful spouse and a healthy home. Danielle and I have been married for almost 22 years. We have three wonderful children. We live in a beautiful town. We are very blessed. Everyone has challenges in family life, and we have certainly had our share, be it the occasional harsh word, a round or two of finger-pointing, petty arguments, confrontations. Even so, we have always done well at resolving conflict. Our children learned at a young age how to take responsibility for their mistakes, and how to give and receive forgiveness. We all work through things; we find our way. Separation is out of the question, divorce unimaginable. I can honestly say our marriage has never been severely threatened. Except once.

About 10 years ago, Danielle found her voice as a leader and started using it. Not a voice of complacent agreement or nominal support, but a unique vibration that originated in heaven and stemmed from the deepest part of her.

Danielle was engaging God in His glorious realms, and her encounters with Him were changing her. She was being awakened to her potential. She was fighting against limitations and taking a stand about people and matters that needed help and attention. And she was speaking up. Frequently. Boldly.

Danielle had received her summons to be Woman, and she wholeheartedly said yes. She was no longer saying what she thought we'd like to hear, and she was not asking for permission. Danielle was becoming Woman in the fullness of her identity, and she was going after everything God had planned for her.

I struggled with this change, every bit of it. I had been accustomed to a wife who mostly followed and rarely led. A dutiful companion who accepted most of my decisions and didn't make waves. She loved me and wanted to be with me, but due to her newfound intimacy with Jesus, she didn't need me in the same way. She valued me but did not depend on me.

Danielle was unafraid to speak her mind, not only at home but also at the church we were leading. She challenged erroneous mindsets and bad attitudes. She insisted on forthrightness and honesty in communication. Moreover, she had fresh vision for change. She was dreaming big dreams and laying the groundwork for ventures she would undertake without my direct involvement.

Danielle found her voice and wings. She was speaking up and soaring high. She would not do as she was told; she would not submit to her husband simply out of fear or respect for his position as Man. Our relationship now had to change, becoming one that was more honoring of Danielle and her process. One that recognized who she truly was in God.

Deep down I knew this was good for Danielle. And I recognized that the change would benefit our marriage and family. But in the course of daily life, I struggled to accept what was happening. I reacted badly. I became angry. I wanted things to go back to normal. It was a difficult time, perhaps the only time Danielle and I contemplated whether we were suddenly incompatible as a couple.

A dear friend—a bold, wise woman of God who serves alongside us—intervened. She spoke with both of us individually. I don't know what she told Danielle, but I'll never forget what she told me: "You need to repent. You must let go of control and manipulation. And you have to submit. To God. To your wife. To His plans for her life and for your marriage." I didn't like it at first, so I took it to God. I didn't inquire of Him—I complained. "I want my wife back!" I said during one of my rants.

The Father's response came swiftly, and it settled the matter for good: "She was never yours to begin with. If you give her to me you'll have her. If you try to hold on to her you'll lose her." Just like that, and from the highest authority in the universe, my appeal was denied. I had no wiggle room left. I had to repent and change my mindset and my ways. Danielle belonged to God. She was wonderful. She was powerful. We had assignments together, and she had assignments of her own. I decided I would do whatever it took to support her, even if it meant laying down my dreams on her behalf.

Everything changed after that. Everything improved. And it's been getting better ever since.

More than any gift I can give Danielle, more than any service I can perform at home, more than all the quality time I can spend with her, Danielle values the freedom I afford her to live for God to the fullest and to pursue the desires of her heart for our family and humanity at large.

Harmonious relationships do not operate on the basis of demands, only agreements. Order and effectiveness are not derived from repeated strained references to chains of command and codes of conduct; rather, they are derived from mutual respect and selfless cooperation. 31M and 31W model these values in their relationship. I'm inspired by them, aren't you?

Men and women are very different in their physical and emotional makeup. Each gender reflects aspects of God's nature in its own unique way. We must celebrate these differences as means by which men and women complement each another. We must express honor and respect for what is accomplished by either of us — regardless of how our approaches differ. Most of all, we must come together as a species, men and women alike, to glorify our King and Savior, Jesus Christ. He gives us life and purpose. And He entrusts to us the governance of his eternal and immeasurable Kingdom.

EPILOGUE

By the time she joined him in bed, he'd been asleep for a good hour and a half. She was careful not to wake him, and for the most part, she succeeded. She changed into bedclothes without turning on the lights, and she slid under the covers stealthily. His back was turned to her, his breathing heavy. She inched up to him and gently ran her fingers through the layers of hair in the back of his head. She propped herself up on her elbow and craned her neck toward his ear. "I love you, babe. I'll go anywhere with you and I'll do anything for you," she whispered.

It wasn't a dream; it was reality. He was enjoying the life of his dreams — a lovely home, a happy wife. He opened his eyes for a brief moment. A smile formed at the corner of his mouth. She couldn't see his face, but she knew he had heard her. She moved in closer.

Before long they were fast asleep in each other's arms. It had been the perfect night for them. They loved deeply. They honored greatly. They drew strength and inspiration from each other continually. And — together — they wrote legacy.

Made in the USA
Columbia, SC
19 August 2018